Materials

Glass

Cassie Mayer

Heinemann
LIBRARY

www.heinemann.co.uk/library
Visit our website to find out more information about Heinemann Library books.

To order:
☎ Phone 44 (0) 1865 888066
▤ Send a fax to 44 (0) 1865 314091
▯ Visit the Heinemann Bookshop at www.heinemann.co.uk/library to browse our catalogue and order online.

First published in Great Britain by Heinemann Library, Halley Court, Jordan Hill, Oxford OX2 8EJ, part of Pearson Education. Heinemann is a registered trademark of Pearson Education Ltd.

Editorial: Diyan Leake
Design: Joanna Hinton-Malivoire
Picture research: Tracy Cummins and Heather Mauldin
Production: Duncan Gilbert

Originated by Chroma Graphics (Overseas) Pte Ltd
Printed and bound in China by South China Printing Co. Ltd

ISBN 978 0 431 19256 7
12 11 10 09 08
10 9 8 7 6 5 4 3 2 1

British Library Cataloguing in Publication Data
Mayer, Cassie
Glass. - (Materials)
1. Glass - Juvenile literature
I. Title
620.1'44

Acknowledgments
The author and publisher are grateful to the following for permission to reproduce copyright material: © Age Fotostock pp. **4** (Targa), **15** (Dinodia); © Alamy p. **5** (Peter Arnold, Inc./Oldrich Karasek); © Corbis pp. **11**, **23** top (Keystone/Martin Reutschi); © drr.net p. **13** (Kenneth M. Jones); © Getty Images p. **12** (Yuka Kisugi); © Heinemann Raintree pp. **7**, **8**, **9**, **14**, **17**, **18**, **19**, **21**, **22** top, **22** bottom, **23** bottom (David Rigg); © istockphoto p. **20** (Maciej Korzekwa); © Shutterstock pp. **6** (Jo Ann Snover), **10** (Semjonow Juri), **16** (David Scheuber).

Cover image used with permission of © agefotostock (Sylvain Grandadam). Back cover image used with permission of © Heinemann Raintree (David Rigg).

Every effort has been made to contact copyright holders of any material reproduced in this book. Any omissions will be rectified in subsequent printings if notice is given to the publisher.

Contents

What is glass?

Glass is something made from sand.
Sand is a natural material.

Glass is made by people.

Glass can be clear.

Glass can be coloured.

Glass can break.

Glass cannot bend.

What happens when glass is heated?

Glass can be heated.

Glass melts when it is very hot.

When glass is heated, it can be made into a new shape.

After it is heated, glass can cool down again.

Recycling glass

Glass can be recycled.

It can be heated and shaped into new glass.

Glass can be used to make
new bottles.

Glass can be used to make new glasses.

How do people use glass?

Glass can be used to make windows.

Glass can be used to make bowls.

Glass can be used to make
light bulbs.

Glass can be used to make lots
of things.

Things made of glass

◄drinking glasses

vases ▶

Picture glossary

melt change from a solid into a liquid. Glass is a material that melts when it is heated.

recycle take old things to make them into new things

Content vocabulary for teachers

material something that can be used to make things

natural material material from plants, animals, or within the earth that can be used by people

Index

Notes for parents and teachers

Before reading   Ask the children to name things in the room made of glass. Discuss what life would be like without things such as windows, spectacles, windscreens, or light bulbs. Talk about the dangers of broken glass.

After reading

• Place eight identical glasses on a flat table. Fill each glass with a different amount of water. Tap the glasses with a metal spoon. Try tapping on different parts of the glass. Can the children find the notes for "Twinkle, Twinkle, Little Star"?

• Show the children examples of stained glass from books or the Internet. Give each child a small rectangle of tracing paper. Tell them to divide up the paper into shapes using a black felt-tip pen and then to colour in the shapes with bold colours. Display the "stained glass" on a window.

• Ask the children to find pictures in magazines of bottles made of different coloured glass – brown, green, clear. Talk about recycling glass and sorting it into different colours before recycling.